FRANCES THOMAS was born in Wales, where she now lives, having spent many years in London. She has written various books for adults and children, including a biography of Christina Rossetti. She has won the Welsh Arts Council's Tir na nOg prize four times for her children's books. She has also written two 'poetry journals', *A Bracelet of Bright Hair* and *Dancing in the Chequered Shade*. Her most recent work is the *Girls of Troy* quartet, published by SilverWood Books. For more information, visit her website at www.francesthomas.org.

Partial Remission

*Poems by
Frances Thomas*

SilverWood

Published in 2023 by SilverWood Books
SilverWood Books Ltd
14 Small Street, Bristol, BS1 1DE, United Kingdom
www.silverwoodbooks.co.uk

Copyright © Frances Thomas 2023

The right of Frances Thomas to be identified as the author of this work has been asserted in accordance with the Copyright, Designs and Patents Act 1988 Sections 77 and 78.

All rights reserved. No part of this publication may be reproduced, stored in a retrieval system, or transmitted in any form or by any means, electronic, mechanical, photocopying, recording or otherwise, without prior permission of the copyright holder.

ISBN 978-1-80042-260-5 (paperback)

Page design and typesetting by SilverWood Books

Partial Remission

*Harriet
(1968 – 2021)*

Contents

Crossroads	13
My Father's Voice	14
Fields	15
The Milkmaid	16
A Bird in the Hand…	18
Heatwave	19
Blue Geraniums	20
The Desolate Fox	21
Wasp Nest	22
Devon	23
This Autumn	24
Pomegranate Seeds	25
Artemesia	27
Kharushere	28
She Spurns His Dreams and His Embroidered Cloths	29
The Fly	30
Three Poems for 2020 (*Rain, The Year When Truth Died,*	32
New Year's Eve)	33
Partial Remission	34
X-Ray	35
Friday Afternoon	36
Poet	37
A Monument	38
Linus, the Neighbours' Cat	39
The Champion	40

Cleaning the Silver	41
No Word for Blue	42
Samuel Palmer – a Cornfield by Moonlight	43
Just Pause Up There…	44
Gloves on a String	45
Halloween Storm	46
Three Haiku	47
Unknown Road	48
For Those Who Have Lost Daughters	49
Afterword	51

PARTIAL REMISSION

Crossroads

I knew it from some other dream
That windswept place where
Roads gathered, met, moved on.
Which way to go? I knew it once
But as I looked, all melted, faded, disappeared.
Was this where she worked? I'd been before
But now she wasn't here. I should phone, perhaps
If only I knew the number.
There were shops here, familiar yet strange.
I didn't go inside; had nothing to buy.
I could get a bus home; buses were everywhere,
Only the numbers were different.
Should I persist in trying to find her?
Would the door be there, and she emerge smiling?
Or would she be a child again, reaching for my hand?
I think one day, I'll find that corridor, that door,
And open it; but I won't be alive.

My Father's Voice

My father was a valley boy, nine in a terrace house;
There were soft green hills, though the river ran choked
 with coal.
He hated the black Sundays, chapel three times,
And an ill-tempered God. But he liked the hymns,
Cwm Rhondda, Calon Lân, Gwahoddiad.
Had a soft light tenor voice and sang them well.
Always with a descant. Who had taught him that?
He left the valleys, soon as he could,
Came to London, lost the accent.
But the voice was there, and when he had a chance to sing,
(Not in church, he had no time for God)
He did so, still with those gentle harmonies.

Fields

The hedge over the hill
Lies like a light ribbon of bronze
Over green-gold fields
Surging to dark woods, or to rushing streams.
Back Field, Thief's Field,
Magpie's Hill, Tom's Pitch,
Claw deep into earth's bones.
'My land' they say. 'I own that.'
Boundaries stronger than kin:
Steep Field, Field-Behind-The-House,
Arrow Plock, Cae Clover,
And Barebones for the bad lands.
Men fight for those hefted spaces,
Grudges held for ever, never forgotten.
Church Field, Penny Field,
Where the drovers rested,
Welsh Farm, Blacklands;
They are lives and limbs;
They outlast the years.

The Milkmaid

Yes sir, come in. Only don't mind if I get on with my work.
What? A pudding, sir, bread pudding – the master likes it
 and we have lots of bread today,
Like we did that day he came.
What? Just as I was – I thought I'd have to sit, or something,
But he said, no, get on with whatever it is you're doing.
Then he stopped me when I was pouring milk, of all things.
 Yes, do that,
Do that again, he said.

He was a strange one, they all said so,
The way he painted, the things he painted,
Me in my old clothes pouring milk.
What? The light? Yes, I keep this table by the window.
He said, about the light that it was good, it was the way he
 liked it,
The way it falls on stuff, well, it has to, doesn't it, in a kitchen?
But why an old brown bowl, when Madam has such lovely
 china?
He just said, he liked the …texture… he said, and the way
 the light… something…
The way the light somethinged on it.

Oh yes, he was an odd one, always broke, they said
Though he had a wife and kids to feed.

You'd think he wouldn't have been so fussy about what he
    painted,
Madam in her new silk dress that looks so nice,
Or Sir with his gun and his dog…
Not me in the kitchen making a pudding.

Would you care for a mug of milk sir? We have good milk here.
Fresh from the cow this morning.

I mean, you can't just paint light, can you?

A Bird in the Hand…

It had fallen – how?
It should have flown; it was a bird.
Its eye bright, its wing, smashed –probably-
We stood around, talked –what to do?
I couldn't leave it there,
So picked it up, cradled it.
It didn't flinch or flutter,
Looked up at me, its bright eye
Trusting, I thought,
Grey breast heaving softly.
We had cats, I couldn't take it home,
But felt it wanted me to do something.
I talked to it gently, and still it looked up at me,
As though it thought I was someone who knew what to do.
It didn't struggle in my hands, wasn't afraid.
There was a vet around the corner,
I took it in, and left it, hesitatingly,
The door clanged behind me, I imagined the scene,
Some woman's only gone and left a bloody pigeon.
I expect they saw the hanging wing and killed it straight
    away,
Pigeons are ten a penny. But I should have liked to save
This one. It had thought better of me.

Heatwave

The slow day drags on its haunches
Down a river of dust;
Sky crackles and glints like foil;
The sun is unrelenting.
The wheat field barely stirs,
Ears heavy with grain,
Fruit bushes sag and gasp,
Berries rot before they fall.
Tarmac is a black glitter;
But who would travel?
We melt like ice creams.
This is a world gone wrong,
Waiting for cool rainfall,
And the gathered damp of leaves.

Blue Geraniums

Blue geraniums grow along the verges,
Fragile, tentative, reaching for blue sky;
They nestle among cow-parsley, meadow-sweet,
Tall grasses like clouds of whey.

My mother called them 'hedge-grows',
A better word, I think.
They've been here for centuries,
Holding back the roads,
Flowers spilling everywhere,
Growing, climbing, swaying to the wind's music.

But now the cutter crawls up the road,
Clanking, grunting, claws outstretched,
Grasses vanish in a pollen cloud.
Geraniums scatter their fragments of sky
Over tarmac. The machine chugs on.

The Desolate Fox

The hills are deep
And go on forever,
Fold after fold, into silence.
There is no moon,
But starlight scatters a faint glow.
He runs up and down the road,
With his harsh insistent bark,
Up and down, round and round, and back again.
He's outside our window now,
We can't see him, but we know he's there.
He goes on and on and on,
Calling into dark silence.

Wasp Nest

Little striped warriors,
All summer you built it,
Your palace of air and paper
Chewed into creamy swirls,
Under my window, and now it's done.

So fly away now, in all your golden armour...
Down to the stream, to the woods, to the hill,

Take your poisoned lances, your strident rage,
Spread fear all around you,
Anywhere, just get away from here.

Don't come into my room, little ones,
You worked so hard,
Built so lovingly and long,
But I'll have to kill you.
There are just so many of you.
So many of you.
I have to kill you.

Devon

This is the fat land, this;
Hills packed tight as a basket of eggs,
Fields green and gold,
Hedgerows dazzle with blossom
Leaves cluster extravagantly.
Cows are cows on a china plate.
Devon! Even the name
Clogs in the mouth like a cream bun

This Autumn

Cloud takes up the mountain in a fist,
Squeezes it dry so that rain streams down the road in a black river.
Scanty trees sway and drop pale leaves,
The wind shakes everything it can get hold of.
Mushrooms rot in the ground.
A spring frost killed all the blossom,
So we have no golden apples-
Something is killing all our rowan trees,
Dying hornets batter our window like little gold missiles.
Even the slugs are…well, sluggish.
The earth is melting and filling up with itself.
They say it's here to stay.

Pomegranate Seeds

When first she arrived, she simply wept,
Soaked her pillow with tears.
What should I do? I loved her so;
A god's love should be enough.
I found her jewels from the deepest depths,
Emeralds, sapphires, opals flashing fire;
Their colours stained the darkness of my walls;
Slaves mined silver, wrought curious bracelets;
Girls like these things.
But still she wept.
Called for her mother. I am your mother now, I said,
Your sister and your brother, you need none but me.
Then she grew hungry, but kept her lips tight shut;
(She knew the score.)
I sent out into her world for them,
Pomegranates, glowing, tawny rose
Piled in their bowl like hot coals.
I envied her the tasting ;
She held the seeds in her hand, rubies against the dark,
Inhaled their scent, could not hold out.
The juice ran down her chin, stained her fingers.
Six seeds, a month for each.
She must stay with me now.
I am not unkind; give her all she can want.
I can comfort and console,

My touch can be fire, or satin,
Golden couches, heaped jewels, scents in crystal vials,
It is all before her. She need not mind the darkness,
I make it light for her.
A thousand thousand slaves attend her every whim.

And yet she will not love me.

Artemesia

A woman? Painting?
Where is the softness, the sweetness, the care,
In those fiery eyes, those brawny arms?
And what she paints, such horrors,
Knives plunged into flesh, blood spurting, staring eyes…
Does she hate men so? What
Have they done to her?
No daughter of mine —
I'd kill her first.
A woman, painting!

Kharushere

(Doorkeeper of the House of Amun, whose mummy is in the Metropolitan Museum, New York)

When he broke bread
The world was fresh and clear as a young leaf,
A god simply a larger sort of person;
As he lit flames, the veil lifted
And the ground cracked with joy.
One day, the Eye blinked, and he was dead.
In the darkness the waters moved. They packed him up,
Tight as a nut, and wrote the symbols of his name.

So how in the world, then, did he fetch up here,
Propped behind glass, in his herringbone shroud,
Four coffins neatly ranged like a Russian doll?

All's different here, in the city of the skies,
Death's a blind mouth and no book tells the way.
He's just a spook, a joke, a Hollywood horror-show.

Bones and black flesh, he's lasted out
For longer than he dared imagine,
But still Eternity's a while away, and he
Must face them out, the long bleak centuries,
His body pining for its final rest.
How could he have known that Time, that careless dustman
Simply unhallows the dead? To this survival
Might he not have preferred the slave's oblivion?

She Spurns His Dreams and His Embroidered Cloths

O, poet, keep your dreams,
Your cloths with stars aglow,
I have my own dreams too,
Which you don't care to know.

You say you want to spread
Those dreams beneath my feet,
You say you'd give me stars,
You beg me to be sweet.

But when you've had your way
You'll vanish like the dew;
You'll find another girl,
To spin those stories to.

So poet, keep your dreams.
I have my own dreams too.
They'll do for me, they'll work for me,
But they won't do for you.

The Fly

As flies go, it's a handsome one, I suppose,
Belly shining blue-green, big, strong.
He lands on my book, and walks tentatively on the edge
    between board and cover,
Stops, then back again, carefully, slow, as if looking for
    something.
Then he lifts off and settles on a shiny patch. (Blake's poems,
    by the way)
He pauses there a long while, then does something delicate
    with his back legs,
Rubbing them against each other, then shaking them out.
    They're so thin, fragile, rickety.
Then stretches out gauzy wings to shake them, then folds
    them back into his body.
He stays there a long while. I don't move either, watching.
Don't want to scare him with my 'thoughtless hand,'
Though in spite of Blake, I do think he's just a fly.
But he's got some pattern, some purpose, which I can't
    discern.
I expect he knows I'm here, but I don't interest him at
    present.
He stays a long time, big eyes staring, wings tucked away,
    is wispy legs quite still.
Then suddenly he shoots into the air, and starts to buzz and
    swoop,

Noisily, annoyingly.
Just another mad buzzy fly after all.

Three Poems for 2020

Rain

It's rained forever, so it seems,
And will rain much more before it ends.
Surely it never rained like this, they say, the world is out
    of joint.
The plague, the fires, the floods,
And that madman in the White House;
Rain is just another thing gone wrong.
And still it's beating down, the sky a soft grey mush,
Sheep huddle in scanty hedges; grass squelches underfoot,
The flowers of summer hang their heads,
While yellow leaves spin drunkenly down.
The world is draining away down the road; when will it end?
And then a robin sings near the window, a carillon of clear
    notes,
As though the sun was shining and the world was new.

The Year When Truth Died

It was the year when Truth died,
When the world, pushed off course by a new plague
Spun helplessly round and round in a darkening sky,
When the palaces of the rich held only madmen;
And lies sparkled so, so glittery and bright
That people exulted in them and went off laughing
As Truth walked off sadly, small and grey, into the void.

New Year's Eve

The snow is still on the hill,
Purpled by the cloud above;
Rooks fly like sharp black crochets.
The unregretted year is history already;
We wouldn't wish it back.
But meanwhile the wind still drags the trees
And dingy sheep feed forever.
I come out of this year an old woman;
And this will not change now.

Partial Remission

We've been together for some time now,
Though you'd hardly know she's there,
In her hidden corner knitting away,
Sharp elbows, feet crossed, clicking, regardless.
Though from time to time, a shoulder tap
And 'You can't do that, dear!'
Until one day – years, months, days, who knows,
I'll feel that tap, the voice less gentle now:
'That's all, dear. You've had enough. Time's up.'

X-Ray

The screen has become a mirror,
My own skull grins back at me.
What does she know? Impossible to tell;
She keeps her secrets locked in bone;
She'll never answer you, she doesn't care.
And if they dig her up some day, they'll find only
She was elderly, Caucasian, female. Bad teeth.
How did she die? She won't say that.
And how she lived?
That, even less.

Friday Afternoon

'It's all clear,' the doctor says. 'You can go.'
It's Friday afternoon. The corridors are hushed, the sky
 outside is mottled grey.
But I walk with a bright step. He's given me Friday evening.
And Sunday, Monday too – all through till next Friday, and
 the Friday next.
He's given me December, the snow on the hills and a holly
 wreath on the door.
He's given me shy snowdrops in the hedge, moon-pale
 primroses
And later the yellow shout of daffodils.

Poet

I met her once.
'Not at all,' she said
As I apologised goofily
For the contact that had put
Her words next to mine.

Words were deep charged for us both,
Though hers flew while mine walked;
Hers took me to places I never visited,
Scaled heights I had no breath for,
Fell scattered like a lapful of petals;
I was entranced by their beauty
Though it could not be mine.
But, just for a moment,
We were companions there.

A Monument

'She hath done what she could,' reads her memorial.
It's a good granite stone – they spent money on it.
And her life was a long one too.
She was a farmer's wife, like most round here.
Her man was fond of her, but never said, till she died,
When he wept uncontrollably, and followed her soon.
Her own dad didn't rate his girls, and she was one of five.
She had children, some of whom died. The vicar told her
    it was God's will.
She listened quietly, but in her heart
Didn't think too much of God for that.
Her grandchildren would laugh at her gnarly hands
    and wrinkled stockings.
Thought she was long out-of-date.
Which she was; the icy dawns of lambing, the bitter winds,
    made up her life,
In moments of rest, she read romances,
Stuffing them down the sofa, so no-body saw.
Her children asked the vicar what to put on her grave;
He struggled to remember her face, but he liked quiet women,
    so he came up with this.

Linus, the Neighbours' Cat

Just an ordinary farm cat,
Big and white and black,
Abandoned, as many are round here, alas,
But found a good home with our neighbours.
Sometimes we meet him half a mile from home.
Half rabbits, dead mice,
He brings them all back, purring;
He's old now, got badly wounded the other day,
(Something fought back)
But still he haunts the verges, waiting.
There are greater and more splendid cats than him in poetry,
Minnaloushe, Jeoffrey, Panguar Ban,
But I feel he has a place among them
For his persistence, his survival,
Against all odds.

The Champion

This was the champion, the butcher proudly said,
First in show, he was.
And I saw the rump and slender flank,
Glass- cased and chilled.
And I thought of how he'd left his world of green,
Bright-eyed and clean, all brushed and fresh,
To a strange new field, among crowds
Led out like a king, praised, garlanded…
To end up in this cold display.
I bought some cheddar cheese, and left.

Cleaning the Silver

This morning, frost ,seen from my window
Made a mountain of silver, a far glimmer;
And I thought of our own silver,
Hidden deep in a cupboard,
I remember my father
Making raw silver shine
And shaping it into treasures.
I bring them out, a jug , a bowl, a jewel box, blackened
    and dull.
But then slowly, under my cloth,
The silver bursts through
Gleaming, pale and radiant,
As the moon emerges from night-time clouds,
Burnishing the clouds with light,
Or like the sheen of frost
Lying on a far hillside.

No Word for Blue

The ancients had no word for blue
Blue was no help for hunters,
Red was blood, or berries; they could be of use.
Rivers were brown, and skies were grey.
Their precious paints were brown or ochre,
Clothes were – well – brown, mostly.
Grass and leaves merged into sky,
The sea was just the sea; surged or was calm.
Homer thought it looked like wine.
There was no blue food (Still isn't, really).
The iridescence of beetles – just something shiny.
Small birds of little interest- and mostly brown anyway.
But when the bluebells came, what then?
When forests surged with blue
And azure waterfalls ran down the hills?
What then?

Samuel Palmer – a Cornfield by Moonlight

That whole day long he'd worked in the hot sun,
Cutting and binding the corn,
Back aching, and hands raw.
But tonight he sees the moon and the evening star ablaze,
Everything washed in light, the shadows sharp as knives.
He takes his stick and goes out into this new ruby and silver world,
his mind tranquil and alert, he could walk forever,
His little dog bounds eagerly by his side;
Wondering why his master has left his fireside and his pipe,
For this dazzling night that looks like day.

Just Pause Up There...

When Nijinsky was asked if it was difficult to do his impossibly high jumps that seemed to hover and stay still in space, he replied 'No! No! Not difficult. You have to just go up and pause a little up there...'

A poem – even this one – is a leap into air,
The clear high space where the poem takes shape.
The Leonardo angel, or a Turner sky,
That top C in the *Miserere*,
Or when Emily Dickinson writes of love,
All come from that high space,
Where nothing was before,
Where the air is gaspingly thin
And the stars crackle and blaze,
And even the birds don't sing.

The poem is made,
The music soars,
The paint glows.
And the dancer pauses in space.

Gloves on a String

Oh those icy childhood winters,
Frost flowers on the windows,
Chilblains and chapped thighs.
Hugging your arms for warmth;
And then the walk to school, crossings and pavements,
A gaberdine mac, a knitted hat,
Long socks and gloves-on-a-string;
Because someone knew,
That it's the nature of gloves to be lost,
And hands to get cold – a small kindness
In unkind days.

Halloween Storm

A kite slices through the sky ,gold leaves hurtle down.
The sun comes out and spills light on the hill,
Then goes away again and the grey cloud wins.
Rivers run fast and brown;
In a village not far away people are drowning.
The ghosts will lie quiet in their spaces tonight,
And I sit with Middlemarch on my lap
Keeping the world outside,
Pretending the storm and the darkness aren't there,
And my only sorrows
Are Dorothea's.

Three Haiku

London dawn...
A bus whines,
A crow squawks,
The sky pales.

Daytime moth;
Just a breath
Of white and gold.

Rain beats down all night.
In the morning a heron stands
Dazed on the shining road.

Unknown Road

We live, so the satnav says
On an unknown road,
Goes from nowhere to nowhere,
Why would you be here?
The hills don't answer,
The birds fly quickly past.

But you'll never find out where the road goes,
Or how long it'll take,
Or where you'll end up,
And who won't be there with you…

For Those Who Have Lost Daughters

… She's briefly in sight
At the turn of the stair,
Just the swirl of a skirt
And the toss of bright hair.

You can still hear her voice,
Loving and mocking,
But there's nobody there.

You struggle to hear,
But your unanswered question
Goes cold in the air

And you're still in the world,
And the light isn't there.

Afterword

'Pomegranate seeds' and 'The Milkmaid' first appeared in *Whirlagust 3* published by The Yaffle Press in 2021.

I'd like to thank Richard, Rob and Beryl for their help and advice in composing these poems.

And just to whisper to the spirit of our late daughter,
Wish you were here…'

The Girls of Troy

Book 1
Helen's Daughter

Hermione has been thrown out by her father Menelaus, king of Sparta, and sent to stay with her uncle Agamemnon at Mycaenae... Hermione's mother Helen, the most beautiful woman in the world, has eloped with Paris, the young prince of Troy, and at present Menelaus can't even bear to see his daughter.

Book 2
The Burning Towers

Troy was once a peaceful and beautiful city but ever since Queen Helen of Sparta abandoned her husband and daughter for the Trojan prince Paris, the Greek armies led by Agamemnon of Mycenae, have been waging war on Troy. Troy's champion is the dazzling Hector, eldest son of King Priam, but the Greeks have the great warrior Achilles. Who will be victorious?

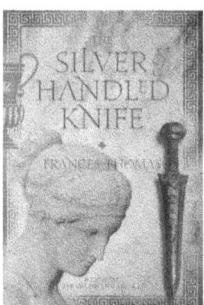

Book 3
The Silver-Handled Knife

Electra is eagerly looking forward to her father Agamemnon's triumphant return to Mycenae after the long war in Troy. But his wife Clytemnestra and her lover Aegisthus have other plans... and suddenly Mycenae isn't a safe place for Electra or her brother Orestes.

www.ingramcontent.com/pod-product-compliance
Lightning Source LLC
LaVergne TN
LVHW041310080426
835510LV00009B/939